I0150291

Teaching and Facilitating Retreats with Caesar

Teaching and Facilitating Retreats with Caesar

A Guide to *Caesar Ate My Jesus: A Baby Boomer's Reflection on Spirituality in the American Empire*

Meg Gorzycki

RESOURCE *Publications* · Eugene, Oregon

TEACHING AND FACILITATING RETREATS WITH CAESAR
A Guide to *Caesar Ate My Jesus: A Baby Boomer's Reflection on Spirituality in the American Empire*

Copyright © 2017 Meg Gorzycki. All rights reserved. Except for brief quotations in critical publications or reviews, no part of this book may be reproduced in any manner without prior written permission from the publisher. Write: Permissions, Wipf and Stock Publishers, 199 W. 8th Ave., Suite 3, Eugene, OR 97401.

Resource Publications
An Imprint of Wipf and Stock Publishers
199 W. 8th Ave., Suite 3
Eugene, OR 97401

www.wipfandstock.com

PAPERBACK ISBN: 978-1-5326-3828-2
HARDCOVER ISBN: 978-1-5326-3829-9
EBOOK ISBN: 978-1-5326-3830-5

Manufactured in the U.S.A.   SEPTEMBER 28, 2017

Contents

Chapter 1

The Curriculum

General Objectives

Caesar Ate My Jesus is unique because it weaves a narrative with four distinct threads: biography, history, theological commentary, and social criticism. In blending these topics, the author aims to represent how individuals experience their own spiritual journeys, as they daily synthesize experience, theological beliefs, social and political events, and cultural norms, and from time to time reflect upon them. The author hopes that readers may improve their awareness of how their daily experiences are connected to each other, and how each are potent with opportunities for spiritual growth and insight.

As an instructional resource, the objectives for reading *Caesar Ate My Jesus* are both personal and academic. The personal motivation for reading of this book is to spark spiritual renewal through the examination of personal beliefs, attitudes, values, and habits. It is to explore how American ideas and social norms have influenced one's spirituality for better or worse. The academic motivations to read this book is to explore American beliefs about faith and religion, and to consider their impact on domestic and foreign policy, with special attention to their impact on the most vulnerable populations. Readers are invited to compare and contrast the Kingdom of God and "Caesar's" empire. They will be promoted to think about the meaning, function, and value of political realism, militarism, materialism, and imperialism. This monograph aims to arouse readers' interest in exploring their own prophetic voices, which may be used to leaven the love of God into the world.

This book is useful for courses in both religious and social studies, including course on:

- Religion, the State, and Politics
- Studies in American Culture and Ethics

- Cold War Culture and Religion
- Faith and Secular Life
- Christianity, God, and the American Empire
- Capitalism and Christianity
- The Spiritual Narrative
- The Prophetic Voice in Society
- Faith in Times of Crisis
- Social Justice
- The Kingdom of God in a Pluralistic World
- Baby Boomer's America

Engaging the Student

As the ultimate goal of the text is to promote spiritual renewal through personal reflection and critical thinking about what Caesar's world demands of us. Courses using this book should be designed to offer students abundant time for sharing ideas, reflecting on the experiences and insights of others, and articulating their thoughts. The following presents ideas for maximizing students' understanding.

Previewing

Introducing students to courses and texts helps students create a set of expectations for course work and set their work in a meaningful context. Instructors may preview the text by providing a statement in the syllabus that speaks to the rationale for reading the text and offers tips on how to approach the narrative. Previews may also include an overview of American Cold War history, and commentary on the ideologies that prevailed during and since that time in America. Instructors should remind students that *Caesar Ate My Jesus* is not intended to speak for all boomers, all Christians, nor intended to represent a comprehensive history of the United States.

Previews might also involve a pre-test. In this case, instructors may want to assess students' knowledge of history, religion, economics, politics, and theological lexicon. The pre-test illuminates students' knowledge deficits without generating a grade, and alerts the instructor to what kind of information students might need in order to succeed in the class. Appendix A offers a sample pre-test.

Ice-breakers

Since class discussions could become very personal and emotional, instructors may want to help students build familiarity and trust with each other. Ice-breakers are tools that facilitate this process. One such ice-breaker, the agreement circle, asks students to stand and move themselves to various positions according to whether they strongly agree (at the center of the circle) or strongly disagree (far from center), and anywhere in between relative to their feelings about each statement. These statements should be general and may include:

- I was raised in a religious household
- I believe in God
- I have struggled with my family's faith
- I believe the Bible should be taken literally
- I have changed my religion at least once in my life
- On matters of public policy, people should keep religion out of the conversation
- Capitalism is a morally neutral economic system
- War is an immoral action
- For the most part, America has overcome racism
- For the most part America has overcome sexism
- The news media in the U.S. has a strong liberal bias
- I know someone who cheated the public assistance system
- Talking about religion make me nervous
- Someone in my family is a member of a religious clergy or community
- I believe in life after death

While these topics may come up in the course, in the ice-breaker, they serve to illustrate how classmates are similar and different on matters. As a follow-up, instructors may have students generate a set of rule for class debate and discussion that are based on mutual respect.

Close Reading

Close reading requires students to think while they read and to monitor their own understanding of what they read. Instructors can help students engage the text by asking students to compose discussion notes based on their reading. These notes might include chapter section summaries, questions about historical events or theological concepts, or commentary about key assertions in a reading. Students may be asked to compare and contrast the assertions in the text to their own beliefs and ideas.

Close reading may also require students to read critically, and assess he logic, veracity, bias, and relevance of assertions. If the text is one of many texts used in the course, students may also be prompted to synthesize, compare, or contrast the material.

The Lecture

This text is not designed for lectures, but rather, for guided discussion. Yet, students may richly benefit from supplemental lectures. Students, for example, may have limited knowledge about American, world, and Church history, legislation, foreign policy, economics, government agencies, religious doctrines, cultural phenomenon, or biographies of influential people. Lectures may fill in the gaps in students' knowledge and provide insights about how to conduct effective independent research.

Small Group Discussion and Pair-Shares

In groups numbering five or less, and in pairs, students may complete academic work related to the course, or engage in reflection, discussion, and debate. The key to effective group work and pair-sharing is structure and purpose. Small groups and pairs can review summaries of readings, create mind maps of concepts or chronologies of key events; they can provide peer reviews of research papers. In groups, students may analyze or evaluate a contemporary speech, proposed legislation, or Supreme Court decisions, then present findings to the class. They may also be a venue in which students explore their personal responses to the ideas and events presented in the text. Students might also explore their feelings and thoughts, and determine whether they have made erroneous assumptions.

Small groups and pairs provide students with a place to "rehearse" their responses to discussion questions before engaging in class discussion. Small groups that have discussions based on the "round robin" approach typically allow each person to speak briefly to a single prompt. Students may learn more about matters, however, if each person's response had to be followed by at least two questions from others that intended to clarify a point, or inquire as to how the speaker might apply an idea, or how the speaker came to a conclusion.

Mid-Term Dip-Sticking

By repeating the pre-test and ice-breaker, students and instructors have the opportunity to identify growth in students' body of knowledge, and to observe and discuss how the course might be causing some students to shift their thinking or attitudes and why. This exercise may also be a platform for a class discussion or compositions based on personal reflection. It may generate questions about history or theology that need to be addressed in the class.

Information and Formation

Courses that generate credits usually require formal assessment of students' work in order to rate their knowledge and skill. Courses that are largely formative present the challenge of how to assess students' growth in values, reasoning, moral judgement, and spirituality. It is vital for instructors to be clear about what kind of information or declarative knowledge is required of students, and what formative experiences are central to the learning objectives.

In *Caesar Ate My Jesus*, information and declarative knowledge pertains largely to facts surrounding historical events, biographies, theological and political lexicon, demographic statistics, and references to film, literature, and music. Instructors are encouraged to hold students accountable for knowing these details as they are the basis of so much commentary. Instructors may enrich their lessons by exploring details about and perspectives of the historical narrative that the author did not address. Students should also be able to speak to the credibility and authenticity of sources used in the text.

The formative aspects of *Caesar Ate My Jesus* are less transparent than the declarative knowledge. The formative concerns the values reflected in the author's assertions and what the author's experiences taught the author about spirituality, morality, and living in Caesar's world. The author's commentary provides readers with the opportunity to reflect on why they either share or do not share the author's values, interpretations, or conclusions, and then to consider the implications of their positions. The goal of such exploration is help students clarify refine their values and what their own experiences have taught them about spirituality, morality and living in Caesar's world.

Many students feel anxious about compositions based on personal opinions because they fear being judged. Some believe that since their reflections are not "hard academic products," (such as that of a research paper), they should not be graded on organization, spelling, grammar, or use of citations. The best approach to grading formative essays and class discussions is to decide what standards and criteria will be considered in such assessment long before class begins, so that these things may be clearly communicated to students on the first day of class. Since personal reflections are subjective in nature, it is helpful for students to know what types of information to include in their work, what elements of composition will be factored into the grade, and why these criteria matter. The following sample represents a statement for a syllabus for the course "Christianity and the American Empire."

Sample Syllabus Statement

> Students' essays and reflections will be graded against criteria that includes clarity of thought, organization, mastery of grammar and spelling, use of evidence, formatting, depth of thought, and originality in thought. By using these criteria, the instructor hopes to improve students' ability to articulate complex ideas and present information in ways appropriate in the academic setting. These criteria reflect this institution's mission that speaks to building competencies in moral development, critical thinking, and scholarly articulation. By considering the depth and originality in thought, the instructor hopes to foster reflections in which students confront their assumptions about others, ambiguity of right and wrong, and the consistency of their own values and behavior.

Sample Rubric

Providing students with sample rubrics enables them to steer research and/or compositions in the right direction. Rubrics are also teaching tools that help students explore examples of compositions and what constitutes the difference between exemplary work, good work, and mediocre work. The following rubric includes assessment elements and assessment criteria.

Rubric for Evaluating Reflection Papers: Each Composition is 25 Points

Criteria	Exemplary (5 pts)	Strong (4 pts)	Sufficient (3 pts)	Emerging (2 pts)
Clarity	Clear main ideas; purpose of essay is transparent; lexicon is well-used; highly original thesis and insights	Main ideas and purpose are largely clear; lexicon is mostly well-used; some profundity in insight noted	Ideas and purpose are generally clear; mastery of lexicon is emergent; originality and insight emerging	Main ideas and purpose of essay are vague or confusing; lexicon is not well-used; lacks original thinking
Organization	Excellent logic in sequence of discussion; strong topic sentences consistently followed by robust and relevant supports	Good logic in sequence of discussion; mostly strong topic sentences largely followed by relevant supports	Emerging logic in sequence of discussion; adequate topic sentences; support are somewhat relevant	Confusing logic in sequence of discussion; weak topic sentences; lacks support and may rely on redundancy
Depth	Outstanding consideration of each aspect or facet of issues or ideas; carefully analyzes broad spectrum of perspectives and possibilities with abundant commentary	Considers more than one aspect or facet of issues or ideas; explores narrow range of perspectives and possibilities with some analysis and commentary	Notes more than one aspect or facet of issues or ideas; notes very few perspective and possibilities, with little analysis or commentary	Lacks awareness of multiple aspects or facets of issues or ideas; lacks analysis of various perspectives and commentary is unsupported, or missing
Originality	Consistently offers fresh insights and original synthesis of information and ideas; reflects a profound mastery of subject	Offers some fresh insights and some original synthesis of information and ideas; reflects a good understanding of subject	Offers one or two fresh insights or original synthesis of information and ideas; grasps general subject on the surface	Offers no fresh insights and no original synthesis of information and ideas; repeats only what others have said and misrepresents some ideas
Mechanics	Impeccable mastery of grammar, spelling, formatting, use of sources and citations	Overall, grammar, spelling, formatting, use of sources and citations is good with few minor errors	Frequent minor errors in grammar, spelling, formatting, use of sources and citations	Lacks understanding of grammar, spelling, formatting, use of sources and citations; many serious errors

Chapter 2

Caesar by Chapter

An Overview

Caesar Ate My Jesus addresses a broad spectrum of events and ideas that have impacted and continue to impact both individuals and society as a whole. It draws readers into American history through personal reflection and an analysis of the spiritual experience as an important part of the human experience. Chapters 1 provides an introduction to and rational for the book. It also acquaints readers with the author's use of key terms found throughout the text. Chapter 2 explores the concept of the Kingdom of God, and examines the political and theological conflicts concerning matters such as the biblical canon, the identity, crucifixion, and resurrection of Jesus, and evolution of the institutional church. In this chapter, readers are introduced to Peter's paradigm, and how it differs from the Gnostic understanding of the Kingdom of God.

Chapters 3–13 offer readers the opportunity to explore American history and culture. They examine the meaning of events, and provide new ideas or insights into existing narratives about the past. These chapters explore the disparity between the nation's espoused Christianity and its conduct at home and abroad.

Chapter 14 reviews the struggle to activate the Kingdom of God and other spiritual teachings in the American empire, and offers ideas about what we might do to renew our spirituality. It challenges readers to confront cynicism and spiritual lethargy, and the way they may have assimilated Caesar's values and agenda. It offers a pathway to hope about the potential of love in our lives.

Each chapter contains assertions may that become the framework for journal writing or essays that address the ways individuals envision their role in bringing the Kingdom of God to bear in the world, or to overcome Caesar in their own personal ways. In addition, each chapter provides material that may be foundational to research. Appendix B offers a list of resources that may be useful for research projects.

Caesar Ate My Jesus may be used in courses in two ways:

- As the core reading. *Caesar Ate My Jesus* is useful to courses that study social and political ethics, and the personal spiritual narrative. A typical college course consists of 15–16 weeks of study. This book contains 14 chapters, and so it can be studied in its entirety in one semester.

- As supplemental reading. *Caesar Ate My Jesus* is useful in studies of contemporary American history or ethics that engages students in the examination of discrete issues and events.

Preparing the Reader for the Content

Prior to undertaking a study of the author's assertions about various American ideas and historical events, it is important for instructors to clarify some basic information. Students should be able to answer the following questions:

1. What is the purpose of the book?

2. What is the author's background and what factors contribute to her credibility?

3. How does the author use the terms: "prophetic voice," "Peter's paradigm," "spirituality," "the Kingdom of God," "Isaac," "Caesar," and "priestly voice?"

4. What is the author's thesis regarding spirituality?

5. What prompted he author to write about spirituality and the American empire?

General Learning Outcomes for Reading
Caesar Ate My Jesus:

1. Students will describe the values, attitudes, and beliefs that shaped how boomers saw themselves and their place in the world, and explain why so many became angry and cynical as they became adults.

2. Students will identify the threats to spirituality that are embodied in imperialism, materialism, and militarism.

3. Students will explore what wars, social reform movements, and corporate behavior reveal about the relationship between being faithful and being American.

4. Students will explore the function and value of dissent, describe the impact dissenters had on society during boomer's lifetime, and ponder what value it may have in one's own life and current society.

5. Students will compare and contrast the way spiritual teachings have been interpreted and applied to social, political, and economic policies and public activism.

6. Students will explore why open and empathetic conversation among people of all religious traditions is both difficult and important to both America's civic life and spiritual well-being.

Reading Guide by Chapter

The following set of questions may be used as a readers' guide. Instructors may use questions to direct small group discussions followed by class discussions, or as prompts for homework assignments that will be discussed in class. These questions target the chapters' content.

Chapter 1: The Boom and Bust of Spirit (pp. 1–14)

Chapter Objectives

The purpose of this chapter is to introduce readers to what baby boomers were taught about being American and the hope of the world. It is to alert readers to the reality that people are profoundly influenced by cultural norms and ideologies. This chapter defines Caesar, which is key to understanding the text. Readers should understand that Caesar is not only a mindset of greedy and corrupt government and corporate leaders; they should appreciate the reality that all individuals have the potential to be "Caesaresque" in their attitudes, values, and priorities.

Chapter One also introduces readers to the claim that in our world, we are told to serve two masters. This claim is key as the rest of the book will challenge readers to not only to see that two masters vie for their allegiance, but that people are often told that the two opposing masters are actually one and the same. In this chapter, readers will learn the author's argument for engaging in public discourse about spirituality, and why the author believes that silence on the matter places people at risk.

Chapter Lexicon

- Caesar
- Gnostic Gospels
- Canonical Gospels
- Prophetic Voice
- Priestly Voice
- New World Order
- Cold War
- *The Affluent Society*, (John K. Galbraith)
- *The Other America*, (Michael Harrington)

Study and Reflection Questions

1. Describe what boomers were promised relative to the material world and why, even at the time of their youth, there were problems with the promises.

2. Explore how the promises of material prosperity impacted American values in the 1950s and 1960s.

3. Explain why living in an empire can present a real spiritual crisis or threaten spirituality.

4. Define the author's understanding of Caesar and Caesar's agenda, and contrast it with sacred teachings about the purpose and meaning of life.

5. The author claims that we need to know about various faiths to speak intelligently about them, so that our criticisms of them are not "hollow and cheap" (p. 11–12); what does this mean?

6. Explore the aspects of Caesar that resonate with your own experiences of American culture, and which do not.

Chapter 2: The Kingdom of Controversy (pp. 15–31)

Chapter Objectives

The purpose of this chapter is to acquaint readers with the concept of the Kingdom of God, and to help them understand the complexity of its origins and meaning. Readers should be able to describe in general the origins of the canonical Gospels, and how they differ from the Gnostic texts. They should also be able to describe the orthodox views of the crucifixion and resurrection of Jesus, how they contrast with other interpretations of the same events, and explain how interpretations of scripture impact the way we see God and others.

Chapter Lexicon

- Kingdom of God
- Essenes
- Peter's Paradigm
- Arianism
- Constantine
- Council of Nicaea
- Literalism vs. Metaphoric Reading of Scripture
- Theocracy

Study and Reflection Questions

1. Identify the notions Jews held about the Kingdom of God at the time when Jesus was preaching; explore the implications and significance of their lack of consensus.

2. Discuss what the evolution of the biblical canon and Church hierarchy reveal about the relationship between sacred wisdom, religious doctrine, and politics.

3. Compare and contrast the Gnostic and orthodox views of the crucifixion and resurrection of Jesus.

4. Identify the social and political advantages and disadvantages of theocracy.

5. Explore the merits and limitations of Peter's paradigm and why as it applies to spirituality.

6. The author notes on page 24 that, "The cross seemed to damn me at the same time it redeemed me." What does the author mean and why might this be a crisis for the faithful?

7. Explore the author's discussion of ego and eternity on pages 25–26, and examine your thoughts about the ego, eternity, and the Kingdom of God and how you personally relate to them.

Chapter 3: The Military Industrial Crucifix (pp. 32–46)

Chapter Objectives

Chapter Three presents readers with an overview of militarism and nationalism that attended the U.S. victory in World War II, and that prevailed throughout the Cold War. The goal is to describe the certainty with which Americans defined their role in the world, and their quickness to justify force for the sake of a "good cause." This chapter introduces the Central Intelligence Agency (CIA) and its covert activities early in the Cold War. It challenges readers to evaluate the assertion that America is a Christian nation.

Chapter Lexicon

- Harry Truman
- Robert Oppenheimer
- American Realism
- Communism
- Isaac (as a metaphor and in the story of Abraham and Isaac)
- Aqedah
- Just War
- Military Industrial Complex
- Nuclear Arms Race
- Dwight Eisenhower
- Eisenhower's Iron Cross

Study and Reflection Questions

1. Describe how the author sees the difference between the Aqedah and Caesar's sacrifices of Isaac, and identify the potential Isaacs in Caesar's world.

2. Identify the Just War theory and principles, and explain why the Cold War may or may not have been just.

3. Debate whether President Truman or President Eisenhower had a more prophetic voice and why.

4. Explore the merits and limitations of realism as a political "ideology," and how these merits and limitations were manifest in the early years of the Cold War.

5. On pages 45–46, the author imagines President Barak Obama making a speech he never made on America's Christian identity; discuss the salience and value of the imagined speech.

6. Identify the early activities of the CIA and discuss whether they enhanced democracy, augmented the wealth and power of Caesar, and leavened the Kingdom of God into the world.

Chapter 4: Pope John Kennedy (pp. 47–64)

Chapter Objectives

The purpose of *Chapter Four* is to explore the idealism of John F. Kennedy, the ways in which Caesar impacted John F. Kennedy, and how John F. Kennedy confronted Caesar in his own ways. It is also to document the impact of his assassination and what public reaction to his death reveals about hope and leadership. The chapter posits that American democracy may not be so democratic.

Chapter Lexicon

- Stained Glass Ceiling
- U.S. Steel Conflict
- Bay of Pigs Invasion

- Cuban Missile Crisis
- National Security Action Memorandum (NSAM) 263
- Warren Report
- Magic Bullet Theory
- John F. Kennedy
- Richard Nixon
- Lyndon B. Johnson
- Nikita Khrushchev

Study and Reflection Questions

1. Identify what the author's description of Kennedy and his political peers reveals about the nature of power in the U.S., and discuss the extent to which the nature of power is this transparent in society, and whether that transparency matter to our spirituality.

2. Explore John F. Kennedy's confrontation of corporate executives and generals in the Pentagon and what it suggests about who controls America's agenda and how consensus is developed.

3. What role did empathy play in the resolution of the Cuban Missile Crisis? Do you believe empathy could play a larger role in solving current political and militaristic conflicts? Explain.

4. The author wrote, "It seems as if the young executive was maturing while in office and growing into the skin of a prophetic leader, reminding us that the Kingdom of God does not emerge whole in any single generation, but evolves, one insight and one judgment at a time." (p. 61); explore the meaning of this statement and its implications for leadership.

5. Describe why John F. Kennedy's assassination was so traumatic from a spiritual perspective, and explain why public reaction to his death and the Warren Report were pivotal in American history.

6. Examine and discuss the reasons why government conspiracies might be spiritual matters.

Chapter 5: The Quicksand of Vietnam (pp. 65–82)

Chapter Objectives

The objectives of *Chapter Five* are to review the motivations for and consequences of the war in Vietnam, and to consider the moral and spiritual implications of American conduct in the war. The chapter invites readers to think about the assertion that the U.S. had to destroy a society in order to save it. The author explores how executive power, reason, and judgment are subject to one's conceptualization of manhood. The chapter introduces a "theology" of war in Vietnam.

Chapter Lexicon

- Great Society
- Mythic Dimension of War
- National Security Action Memorandums, 52, 273, 273
- Gulf of Tonkin Resolution
- My Lai Massacre
- Vietnam Syndrome
- "The Least of My Brothers"
- Theology of the Vietnam War
- Henry Kissinger
- William Westmoreland
- Robert McNamara
- Ho Chi Minh
- Dien Bien Phu
- Ngo Dinh Diem
- *Retrospect* (Robert McNamara)

Study and Reflection Questions

1. Trace the U.S. involvement in Vietnam from 1945 to 1975 and identify the various motivates for military intervention; discuss the role of ego in policy-making and what it reveals about leadership.

2. Identify the incentives the government has for withholding information about war from the people, and address the implications of this for both democracy and morality.

3. Explain why America's war against Ho Chi Minh was ironic in some ways.

4. Describe the American treatment of Vietnamese civilians—including women and children—and discuss what this reveals about human dignity, and the American concept of manhood.

5. Describe the conditions and experiences that led to Vietnamese resistance of the American agenda.

6. Identify the author's the theological lessons of the war in Vietnam, and explore how they might speak to Americans a present.

Chapter 6: Dissent (pp. 83–105)

Chapter Objectives

The purpose of *Chapter Six* is to explore the continuity of dissent in American history, and demonstrate its relationship to faith and spirituality. This chapter confronts the myth that dissenters are largely ignorant and anti-American people who lack a moral compass. The goal of this chapter is also to foster an awareness of the fact that not all dissent is noble, and that activism on behalf of liberal and conservative causes are both vulnerable to Caesar's influence. The text explores the power of media, and the tension between selling spectacles and providing thorough information and sound analysis.

Chapter Lexicon

- Dissent
- *Winchester Victory*
- Anti-War Movement

- *Einstein-Russell Manifesto*
- Anti-Nuclear Movement
- Pentagon Papers
- Prior Restraint
- Fulbright Committee
- Democratic National Convention, 1968
- Test Ban Treaty
- Students for a Democratic Society
- Daniel Ellsberg
- Kent State Massacre
- Clergy and Laymen Concerned about Vietnam
- Union of Hebrew Congregations
- Daniel and Philip Berrigan
- Cardinal Spellman
- Thomas Merton
- Pope John XXIII
- Port Huron Statement
- *Pacem in Terris*

Study and Reflection Questions

1. Describe the opposition to atomic bombs and its links to the Ant-War Movement.

2. Explain why the first protests against the Vietnam War were generally peaceful, and explain why violence and hostility in protests escalated in the late 1960s and early 1970s.

3. Explore what the reactions of presidents and their advisors to protests against the war in Vietnam and what they reveal about the government's respect for public opinion.

4. Identify the reasons why many on both sides of the war in Vietnam saw it as a moral issue.

5. Reflect upon and discuss the way secular and religious leaders justified the war in Vietnam, and what this reveals about the struggle to integrate one's spiritual life with one's civic life.

6. Explore what prevents people who disagree with "Caesar" from dissenting, and how some obstacles might be overcome.

7. Explain how it is possible for egos to sabotage peace and reform movements.

8. Explain why the Democratic National Convention in Chicago, 1968 was a significant event.

9. Discuss the differences between selling sensation and spectacle and providing thorough news and information with sound and in-depth analysis, and explain why the former so often prevails.

10. Discuss the meaning and merits of the statement: "When a 9-year old undergoes a shift from having complete trust and faith in leadership to being cynical by age 16, it is a contained crisis that threatens one individual's maturation process, and confidence in civility. When a whole society undergoes the same shift, it is a collective crisis that threatens the very moral outlook of that society, and undercuts the will of a whole generation to cooperate and make sacrifices necessary for the good of us all" (p. 103).

Chapter 7: Civil Rights (pp. 106–125)

Chapter Objectives

In *Chapter Seven,* readers encounter an overview of the Civil Rights Movement. The purpose of the chapter is to recall highlights of the movement, and to remind readers of the role that faith played in the movement. The text aims to raise the readers' awareness of the contradictions that emerge when those who call themselves "Christian" justify racism and violence against peaceful dissent. The chapter underscores the importance of the stories we hear, as explored briefly in the author's recall of films viewed as a child. The material illustrates the connection between public law and personal morality.

Chapter Lexicon

- Civil Rights Movement
- CORE
- SCLC
- SNCC
- Martin Luther King, Jr.
- Malcom X
- Ella Baker
- Rosa Parks
- NAACP
- Hubert Humphrey
- Civil Rights Act, 1957
- Freedom Rides
- Andrew Goodman
- James Chaney
- Michael Schwerner
- Civil Rights Act, 1964
- Voting Rights Act, 1965
- Segregation
- Minnesota Nice

Study and Reflection Questions

1. Identify the theological roots and religious elements of the Civil Rights Movement, and how spirituality influenced the goals and strategies of the movement.

2. Describe the difference between patronizing people and working for justice.

3. The author notes that Civil Rights workers confronted "third world conditions in their own back yard" (p. 117); explore what that meant and whether third world conditions exist in the U.S today.

4. Identify the author's observations about the ways the Anti-War and Civil rights Movements succeeded and fell short of its political and spiritual potential.

5. Discuss Lyndon Johnson's remarks about giving Negros "just enough to quiet them down" (p. 113), and what it reveals about the American commitment to civil rights and social justice.

6. Identify the price those who used their prophetic voices paid to advance civil rights and social justice, and discuss what this reveals about society's capacity for spiritual maturity.

7. Explore the author's assertions about political correctness and why it is a poor substitute for genuine empathy and love of neighbor.

Chapter 8: Sex and the Kingdom (pp. 126–148)

Chapter Objectives

A brief overview of the sexual revolution of the 1960s and 1970s appears in *Chapter Eight*, and its purpose is to recall some of key shifts in society's thinking about sex and sexuality. Commentary in the chapter is intended to call the reader's attention to perspectives that he or she may not have considered, and to provoke consideration of the extent to which the sexual revolution was morally revolutionary and/or a hedonistic rebellion. The chapter coaxes the reader to think about sexism, sexual violence, and sexuality from the perspective of the vulnerable. The purpose of such thinking is to arouse empathy, and to spark personal inventories of the individual's regard for intimacy, sexual exploitation, sexism, homophobia, and the objectification of the human person.

Chapter Lexicon

- Sexual Revolution
- Feminine Mystique
- Betty Friedan
- Griswold v. Connecticut, 1965
- Roe V. Wade, 1973
- Mary Daly

- Germaine Greer
- Andrea Dworkin
- Kate Millett
- Shulamith Firestone
- Midge Decter
- Phyllis Schlafly
- Baker v. Nelson
- Misogyny
- Miller v. California
- Alfred Kinsey's Studies of Human Sexuality
- Playboy Philosophy
- Hugh Hefner
- President's Commission on Obscenity and Pornography, 1970
- Meese Report, 1986
- Stonewall Riot, 1969
- Harvey Milk
- John Jay Report, 2004

Study and Reflection Questions

1. Explore what the author's experiences as a child reveals about children's sensitivity to sex and their own sexual identity, and discuss some implications for childrearing and education.

2. Identify the ways in which the sexual revolution was a rebellion against responsibility and intimacy, and in what ways was it restorative of human dignity.

3. Determine whether America has experienced a true sexual revolution.

4. Debate whether the censorship of sex in mass media is more or less the responsibility of individuals and parents and why.

5. Describe what the liberation movements for women, gays, and straights different had in common and what made each unique.

6. Explore what the meaning of the author's statement that, "men and women are two genders separated by a common ego" (p. 148), and what it implies about social norms and spirituality.

7. Identify the ways that social and biological sciences might inform theological inquiries and teachings related to sex and sexuality, and speak to the benefits that might be achieved by this.

8. Discuss what it means to have one's sexuality fully integrated into their spirituality.

9. Explore the evidence that supports and refutes the assertion that violent video games and pornography has an adverse effect on those who view these images and play these games, and discuss your beliefs about the spiritual and moral consequences for consuming such material.

Chapter 9: The Dignity of Labor (pp. 149–163)

Chapter Objectives

The purpose of *Chapter Nine* is to guide readers' exploration of the meaning of work in the American economy, analyze the merits and detriments of capitalism, and to explore whether our personal and social beliefs about the market, wealth, and material possessions has a positive or negative impact on our spirituality. This chapter prompts readers to think about where they learned about the dignity of the human person and work. Readers will consider the extent to which their own workplaces are like "Caesar's workshop," and what might be done to leaven the Kingdom of God in those places.

Chapter Lexicon

- America's Ruling Class
- Barbara Ehrenreich
- Rerum Novarum
- *Economic Justice for All* (U.S. Catholic Conference of Bishops)
- Working Poor
- Caesar's Workshop
- Market as God

Study and Reflection Questions

1. What does the author means by the "dignity of labor," and what are the major threats to the dignity of labor in the American society; determine whether you agree and why.

2. Describe what happens to individuals when their sense of dignity in the workplace is diminished, and what happens to a society that treats its members according to an unofficial caste system.

3. Explain how is it possible to be a productive society and yet not prosper as a worker.

4. Reflect on those moments wherein you felt like somebody was treating you like a commodity or when you treated somebody else as a commodity; then, discuss the motives involved in those instances and explore how love of neighbor might have been applied in different ways.

5. Debate whether it is inappropriate or impossible to leaven the Kingdom of God into the workplace.

6. The author states that, "Hawkeye's generosity to us six kids was magnified by her meager earnings, just as Ham's parsimony was magnified by her wealth" (p. 152); explore whether the statement might apply to the United States' relationship with the rest of the world.

7. Discuss Caesar's workshop, how is it different from the Kingdom of God, and why it prevails.

Chapter 10: Banksters and Creditmeisters (pp. 164–178)

Chapter Objectives

The major function of *Chapter Ten* is to explain the evolution of predatory capitalism during boomer's lifetime, and to compel readers to consider the winners and losers of American investment banking and corporate practices. The chapter is also intended to offer insights to how the nation's leaders think about wealth, who deserves it, and why. This material invites readers to question the morality and wisdom of fiscal and business practices, as their consequences are frequently psychological and spiritual, especially for the poor and vulnerable.

Chapter Lexicon

- Official Poverty Level
- Glass-Stegall Act, 1933
- Deregulation
- Speculation
- Financial Products
- Financial Services Modernization Act, 1999
- Commodities Future Trading Commission
- Brooksley Born
- Alan Greenspan
- Federal Reserve
- Mortgage Crisis
- Lobbyist
- Government Oversight

Study and Reflection Questions

1. Describe the shift in the distribution of wealth in boomer's lifetime, and how this distribution was facilitated by legislation and court decisions.

2. Describe the political rhetoric that has been used to justify speculative investments, reductions in taxes for the rich and corporations, and deregulation of banking and industry; and, discuss why the general public is vulnerable to such rhetoric.

3. Identify the crisis Brooksley Born attempted to prevent, and describe how she was treated by her peers; then, discuss what does her story reveals about government over-sight and policy-making.

4. Debate whether the difference between Republicans and Democrats on the matter of investment banking is significantly different, and which is more empathetic to the poor and vulnerable.

5. Determine whether a society that endows corporations with the same rights as individuals risking the integrity of its spirituality and/or moral moorings.

6. Consider the daily work of lobbyists, the amount of public revenue lost because of tax-loop-holes and shelters, the mass profits reaped from war, and the regularity of corruption, and address the question of whether the media is biased in reporting these things.

7. Discuss Senator Marc Rubio's assertion that when the Pope speaks on economic issues, he is not speaking with authority because the subject of economics is not a moral issue (p. 178).

8. Describe America's standards of material wellness, how it differs from people in developing nations, and the poor in the United States, and whether a person's standard of living is a spiritual matter.

Chapter 11: Born Again Caesar (pp. 179–199)

Chapter Objectives

The objective of *Chapter Eleven* is to identify the causes for the revival of Christian fundamentalism in the late twentieth century, describe the secular and spiritual agendas of the Christian Right, and to raise questions concerning whether the Born Again Movement brought society any closer to the Kingdom of God. This material challenges readers to consider the legitimacy of American military interventions that have been undertaken with what leaders believed was God's blessing, and to reflect upon the conduct of American military personnel and the foreign armies they trained.

Chapter Lexicon

- Christian Fundamentalism
- Christian Right
- Christian Coalition
- Theocracy
- Taliban
- Al Qaeda
- Ronald Reagan
- Jimmy Carter
- George H. W. Bush

- Civil Religion
- Jerry Falwell
- Harvey Cox
- Social Darwinism

Study and Reflection Questions

1. Describe the causes and characteristics of the "Born Again" movement of the 1970s, and explain why it was so popular.

2. Define the Christian Right, their political objectives, and debate whether it contributed to the spiritual growth as a nation.

3. Explain why the Watergate scandal was a crisis for both democracy and spirituality.

4. Describe how Presidents Carter, Reagan, G.H.W. Bush, Clinton, and G.W. Bush solicited the Christian Right, and discuss whether they lived up to the Christian Right's expectations.

5. Explore the merits of the quote, "Americans love captains of industry and warriors, but they only tolerate intellectuals, poets, and peacemakers" (p. 190) and discuss the implications of the statement.

6. George H. W. Bush prayed that Americans remember that the only "just use of power was to serve people" (p. 193); determine whether his administration lived up to this prayer.

7. Describe the difference between social Darwinism and the Kingdom of God.

8. Describe the author's critique of "born-again" politicians and debate whether these critiques are fair.

9. Describe the emotional and intellectual tension of which the author speaks on pages 198–199 when addressing the matter of supporting President George H. W. Bush's policies and actions; then, explain why the President's attitudes and actions constitute a spiritual crisis for the author, and discuss whether you agree with the author and why.

Chapter 12: A View from Distant Shores (pp. 200–219)

Chapter Objectives

The goal of *Chapter Twelve* is to introduce readers to salient episodes in American foreign policy late in the Cold War, and invite them to consider the motivates and consequences of U.S. attitudes towards our global brothers and sisters. The chapter punctuates the reality that the call to empathy lives in the details of history. The chapter also prompts readers to consider the differences between liberation theology and traditional orthodox Christian theology.

Chapter Lexicon

- El Salvador Civil War
- Jean Donovan
- Ita Ford
- Dorothy Kazel
- Maura Clark
- Tinhorn Dictators
- Alliance for Progress
- Oscar Romero
- Jose Duarte
- Nelson Rockefeller
- William Ford
- Robert White
- Junta
- Pope John Paul II
- Rockefeller Report
- School of the Americas
- Glasnost
- Perestroika
- George Kennan
- Mikhail Gorbachev
- International Monetary Fund

Study and Reflection Questions

1. Describe how President Kennedy's vision for Latin America differed from corporations and their cold warrior allies.

2. Determine whether the legacy of American intervention in Latin America during boomer's lifetime leavened the Kingdom of God into Latin American society or depleted it.

3. Define liberation theology and explain why the Catholic Church and U.S. government disliked it.

4. Identify the "Isaacs" that were sacrificed by U.S. policy in Latin America from 1945 to 1991.

5. Describe the author's theological problems with Christian fundamentalism and explore whether you share her concerns and why.

6. Trace the collapse of the Soviet Union from 1984 to 1991 and identify activities behind the Iron Curtain that led to the liberation of Eastern European countries.

7. Explain why the author criticizes the assertion that the U.S. won the Cold War, and explain why the way the history is remembered matters.

8. Describe the author's perception of Bush's and Thatcher's treatment of Gorbachev, and explore the implications of their treatment for world order and the world at large.

9. Determine whether Mikhail Gorbachev represented a prophetic voice, and explore why many Americans struggle to embrace his vision for world peace and cooperation.

Chapter 13: Post-Cold War Caesar (pp. 220–241)

Chapter Objectives

The purpose of *Chapter Thirteen* is to acknowledge the continuity of American politicians' Christian rhetoric in the post-Cold War era, and to question whether the rhetoric is aligned with American policy and conduct at home and abroad. This chapter discusses the administrations of America's first two baby boomer presidents, and addresses the September 11th attacks on the World Trade Center and whether American imperialism lives in the twenty-first century despite some obvious conflicts with Gospel teachings.

Chapter Lexicon

- Cultural War
- Bill Clinton
- George W. Bush
- North American Free Trade Agreement
- World Trade Organization
- Globalism
- Rwandan Genocide
- 9/11
- Hurricane Katrina
- Enron
- Osama bin Laden
- Carlyle Group
- Abu Graib
- Clinton Foundation

Study and Reflection Questions

1. Identify the opportunities that post-Cold War presidents had to retreat from empire-building and to pursue global cooperation for peace and prosperity, and determine whether they retreated and why.

2. Determine whether the first boomer presidents served Caesar or brought the Kingdom of God of bear on Earth, and describe their impact on the poor and vulnerable at home and abroad.

3. Describe the benefits and detriments of trade policies with China and Mexico.

4. The author stated, "It seems that at dazzling heights of political power, people stop identifying with the common masses who offer them their trust, and start to identify more with the world's rich and powerful who offer them their favors. At this altitude, fellow countrymen and national borders fade from view, and all that remains are the interests of global aristocracy who no longer identifies with those who are condemned to

struggle for a decent human existence" (p. 229); discuss the veracity and implications of this claim.

5. Debate whether it is necessary for a society to be a democracy in order to bring the Kingdom of God to bear in the world, and whether it is essential for individuals to have civil liberties to bring the Kingdom of God to bear in their lives.

Chapter 14: In Excelsis Deo (pp. 242–257)

Chapter Objectives

The goals of *Chapter Fourteen* are to present the case for hope in humanity and our spiritual potential, and to offer strategies to renew and invigorate our spirituality. This chapter challenges readers to become more introspective and forthright in the assessment of the degree to which they have assimilated Caesar.

Chapter Lexicon

- *A Report on the Governability of Democracies*
- Frog Soup
- Caesar's Treadmill
- Messianic Fatigue
- *The Four Agreements* (Don Miguel Ruiz)

Study and Reflection Questions

1. Identify how it is possible for individuals to confront hopelessness in small but meaningful ways.

2. Define messianic fatigue, what it reveals about our approach to faith, address how it could possibly be detrimental to our moral development and spirituality, and speak to how it can be avoided.

3. Debate the assertion that it is unrealistic and self-defeating for a society to abandon Caesar's goals and methods.

4. Describe the author's critique of doctrine and sentimentality, and its merits and limitations.

5. Discuss the author's thoughts about the certainty with which we know God, and explore why making peace with uncertainty might bring the faithful closer to God.

6. Explain what it means to "get off the treadmill," and why the author regards this as a "sacrament."

7. Explain why the author regards dissent as a vital element in our spirituality, and explore what dissent means to your own spirituality.

8. Explore what it means to be part of an "ecosystem" of love, and whether secular society has an obligation to nurture it.

Chapter 3

For the Historian

Caesar Ate My Jesus addresses many historical events, but the narrative is limited in the scope of details it presents. For that reason, the history instructor may want students to delve deeper into events, so that the complexity of events may become more apparent, and so that students may better understand the causes, consequences, and chronologies of events. Instructors are encouraged to assign research projects that focus students' attention on key episodes in American history, seminal documents, and on the biographies of important figures and organizations. Projects of this nature that are based on the book may augment material presented in the text, deepen the readers' comprehension of history, and improve their ability to synthesize information from multiple sources. The following material offers instructors some options that are organized by chapters in *Caesar Ate My Jesus*.

Chapter 1: The Boom and Bust of Spirit

1. Interview family members or friends who grew up as baby boomers. Describe the world outlook they had as youngsters and how that world view shifted over the course of a life time. Identify the key experiences that impacted their faith, spirituality, and regard for secular leadership, and describe the impact. Explain how their class, race, color, religion, and gender may have influenced their values, attitudes, and experiences.

2. Investigate poverty in America for the first decade after World War II. Identify the causes of poverty and what variables contributed to its persistence. Report the efforts of government and community leaders to alleviate poverty, and describe their successes and failures. Describe the

resistance that they encountered, what motivated resistance to economic reforms, and the way responded to resistance.

3. Research American anti-Semitism or anti-Catholicism during the Cold War. Report findings related to the Jewish or Catholic experience, and describe how Jews and Catholics responded to bigotry against their religion. Offer insights to the American experience of religious anxiety and civil rights, and comment on the scope and limitations of the American dream.

4. Research the status of women in America during the first two decades after World War II. Describe the attitudes of Americans towards women, sexuality, domestic abuse, and reproduction. Describe efforts to advance women's rights and status and how religion was often used to justify women's status. Comment on the scope and limitations of the American dream.

5. Research the status of a racial or ethnic minority in America during the first two decades after World War II. This may include Native Americans, African Americans, Hispanics, and Asians. Describe the attitudes of Americans towards this population and identify the source of these attitudes. Describe efforts to advance the population's rights and who opposed such advancement and why. Comment on the scope and limitations of the American dream.

Chapter 2: The Kingdom of Controversy

1. Research the origins of the canonical Bible. Discuss the theological and political variables that shaped its content. Describe the intentions of officials who made editorial decisions. Describe scholarly concerns about the canon with regard to editing and translation. Identify the texts that were omitted from the canon, and address scholarly concerns about their omission.

2. Create a historical profile of religions and philosophies that thrived in Palestine during the life of Jesus of Nazareth. Describe the common elements of these religions and philosophies and identify their unique features. Discuss the relationship between governance and religion in ancient Palestine

3. Investigate the events that led to the creation of the Nicaean Creed, and describe the religious and political interests at stake. Identify the important leaders who make critical decisions about the document, and what motivated their decisions.

4. Research the Gnostic community that thrived in Palestine at the time of Jesus. Describe their origins, beliefs, and agenda. Identify the leaders of Gnosticism and their sacred texts. Contrast the Gnostic and Jewish approach to faith, and discuss whether Gnosticism was a threat to Jews and why.

Chapter 3: The Military Industrial Crucifix

1. Research the origins of the Cold War. Describe how the traditional American view differs from those of Marxists and revisionists. Identify the events that contributed to tensions between the U.S. and Soviet Union, and how personalities played a role in the emerging conflict. Determine whether the Cold War was largely an ideological conflict or one rooted in nationalism and imperialism.

2. Conduct a study of U.S. history books that are widely used in secondary schools, and determine whether the representation of Cold War events is fair, broad in the scope of perspectives represented, and empathic to various stakeholders in crisis and foreign policy-making. Comment on the implications of findings.

3. Investigate the controversy over atomic bombs in the 1940s and 1950s. Trace the evolution of atomic policy from 1945 to 1955. Identify advocates of a U.S. monopoly and proliferation of stronger weapons, and those who wanted to collaborate with other nations on the regulation of atomic power and limit the creation of new and more powerful bombs. Discuss the motivations for advocates and dissenters of U.S. atomic policy and nuclear proliferation. Describe the consequences of the U.S. atomic policy in terms of cost, public health, and international relations.

4. Study the biography of a key figure in the early nuclear years, (such as Harry Truman, Dwight Eisenhower, John McCloy, Robert Oppenheimer, James Byrnes, Leo Szilard, Edward Teller, Henry Kissinger, Dagmar Wilson, and Bella Abzug), and report their involvement either in the advancement of nuclear weapons or their opposition to them. Identify the ideas and values that shaped their thinking. Describe their role and discuss how they responded to their adversaries.

5. Explore the origins of the CIA and its associations with private interests in the U.S. Discuss the covert operations of the CIA between 1947 and 1960, and identify the potential contradictions between such activity and

the democratic principles for which the U.S. stood. Did the CIA activity mitigate or exacerbate global conflict? Explain.

Chapter 4: Pope John Kennedy

1. Examine the biography of John F. Kennedy and identify the values and experiences that shaped him in his youth. Describe his ascent to the presidency and why this upset political elites and their supporters. Describe how Kennedy's perspective of the Cold War and global leadership evolved while he was in the White House, and why this was a threat to the military-industrial complex.

2. Describe foreign policy during the Kennedy administration, and describe how managing events in Asia had potential repercussions and implications for the Eastern Bloc and Latin America. Determine to what extent Kennedy's policies and actions were driven by personal motivations, political considerations, public perceptions, material resources, and moral obligations.

3. Investigate the news coverage and editorials related to the religion factor in the election of 1960, and discuss what the rhetoric reveals about the degree to which Americans had matured on the matter of religious tolerance. Provide abundant examples and commentary.

4. Research John F. Kennedy's assassination. Trace the events that led to the conclusion that Lee Harvey Oswald acted alone, and identify the evidence that contradicted that assertion. Discuss the motives that the FBI, CIA, banks, and private industries had for killing Kennedy. Explain why the assassination and killer's motives matter to Americans decades after the event.

5. Examine Jim Garrison's On the Trail of Assassins (1988) and Mark Lane's Last word (2011), which were both written after the House Select Committee on Assassinations published their final report (1979), and concluded that conspiracies were indicated in the deaths of John F. Kennedy, Martin L. King, Jr., and Robert Kennedy. Discuss what Garrison and Lane discovered about JFK's murder, the CIA, the Warren Commission, and explore what their efforts to seek and reveal the truth tells us about power in our society.

Chapter 5: The Quicksand of Vietnam

1. Trace the U.S. involvement in Vietnam from 1945 to 1975. Present the arguments in favor of and against escalation of the war in 1965. Explain why various individuals took sides and why one argument prevailed and the other did not.

2. Investigate the cost of the Vietnam War and identify who profited from the war. Identify the conflicts of interest that existed in cases where law-makers had investments with companies that provided the accoutrement of war. Describe the extent to which the American public was aware of these conflicts at the time, and address the implications of such awareness.

3. Research the formation of soldiers during the 1950s and 1960s. Describe the psychological training they received and how this impacted their view of foreigners, patriotism, and their own manhood. Describe the role religion played in the military, and discuss the implications.

4. Study Robert McNamara's thesis found in *The Fog of War* and *In Retrospect*, and identify the key lessons he learned from Vietnam. Determine whether the U.S. learned those lessons in the decades that followed the Vietnam War, and offer evidence for conclusions.

5. Prepare a report on the Fulbright Committee. Describe its origins, its goals, and its outcomes. Identify the advocates and adversaries of the committee and describe their reasons for taking the side they took. Comment on what the Committee teaches policy-makers in the twenty-first century.

6. Research the Vietnamese history of the war in Vietnam and compare it with that of American historical accounts. Explain what the significance of differences might be, and why it is valuable to learn history from the perspective of other nations.

7. Develop a thesis based on the assertion that: "Had it not been for the war in Vietnam, President Johnson would have been re-elected and achieved his Great Society agenda."

Chapter 6: Dissent

1. Research the rise and fall of the Students for a Democratic Society (SDS); describe their objectives and strategies. Identify the leaders of the SDS and describe the values and experiences that shaped their world view. Trace the collapse of the SDS and comment on what this experience teaches subsequent generations about the nature of reform movements and their viability.

2. Compare and contrast the theology of the Christian Right (such as Billy Graham, Jerry Falwell, Cardinal Spellman, and Pat Roberson) and liberal theologians (such as Harvey Cox, William Coffin, Martin Luther King, Jr., and Charles Curran) on a specific topic, such as civil rights, the war in Vietnam, poverty in America, gay rights, feminism, or nuclear weapons. Identify the arguments on both sides. Comment on what religious conflict over the topic reveals about American culture.

3. Research the positions of the Catholic Church during the Cold War on communism and capitalism. What materials interests did the Catholic Church have at stake on the matter of global economics? Describe the key Catholic encyclicals issued during the Cold War, and discuss whether they resonate with American realism, or aspire to something more idealistic.

4. Write a thesis in response to the question: "At what point does dissent become counter-productive and destructive of its own ideals?" Use a specific example from an organization related to the Civil Rights, Feminist, Anti-War, Anti-Nuclear, or Gay Rights Movements to develop the thesis.

5. Conduct an in-depth study of news magazines' news and editorial legacy on a single topic during a given time frame. Determine which approach did more to advance democratic principles and why. Examples of this project include: 1) Compare and contrast *Ramparts Magazine's* and *Time Magazine's* coverage of the 1968 presidential election; or, 2) Compare and contrast *The National Review's* and *The Nation's* coverage of the war in Vietnam from 1963–1969

Chapter 7: Civil Rights

1. Trace the origins of the Civil Rights Movement from 1945 to 1965. Identify the key leaders and the role that religion played in the development of their agenda and strategies. Explain how Christianity was used by proponents and opponents of civil rights. Discuss the implications.

2. Study the biographies of civil rights activists, (such as Robert Moses, Malcom X, Martin Luther King, Jr. Fannie Lou Hamer, Ella Baker, Bayard Rustin, James Farmer, Medgar Evers, and Barbara Jordan), and describe the values and experiences that shaped their activism. Identify their objectives, what barriers they confronted, how they responded to these barriers, and comment on what their lives teach subsequent generations about the relationship between law and human dignity.

3. Research Affirmative Action. Describe its origins, identify its advocates, and report its success and failures. Discuss the current controversy surrounding Affirmative Action and its implications.

4. Trace the history of the Civil Rights Bill of 1964. Identify its advocates and adversaries and their motives. Identify the compromises that were made and why they were made. Address what this experience teaches subsequent generations about the nature of creating legislation in the U.S.

5. Research the investigation of the deaths of Chaney, Goodman, and Schwerner. Address the role of the local sheriff's offices, the FBI, and local citizens. Report the outcomes, and comment on what this experience teaches subsequent generations about criminal justice in the U.S.

6. Investigate the role of the FBI and CIA relative to the Civil Rights Movement. Describe their agendas, their motivations, and discuss their impact on the movement. Discuss what their involvement reveals about democracy, power, and human dignity in America.

Chapter 8: Sex and the Kingdom

1. Investigate the post-World War II cultural propaganda that promoted the cult of femininity. Describe its impact on women's economic and social status. Describe the role of law-enforcement, courts, and the medical and psychiatric community in the enforcement of cultural norm regarding women's place, and describe the consequences of such norms.

2. Trace the development of the birth control pill and describe the reaction to the development by both conservative and liberal religious and secular leaders. Describe the key issues at stake on the matter of women's access to the pill. Discuss the key laws and court cases that led to women's access and why birth control remains controversial at present.

3. Research the Gay Rights movement from 1945 to the present. Describe the conditions that drove gays and lesbians to publically resist harassment, discrimination, and assaults. Identify the key turning points and why they were important. Identify the risks activists took and why they took them. Identify the religious opposition to and the religious support for gay rights and what this reveals about American society.

4. Research and develop a thesis on the question of whether Hollywood films had a positive or negative impact on the sexual revolution in the 1960s and 1970s.

5. Investigate the evolution of public awareness about domestic abuse and rape, and report how and why attitudes, policies and laws have changed since 1945. Discuss the roles of the medical community, public education, the media, and religion in the perpetuation of violence against women.

Chapter 9: The Dignity of Labor

1. Investigate the history of labor from 1945 through the present. Discuss the conditions that led to labor unrest and labor reform. Note key legislation and address their significance. Identify the opponents of labor unions and labor rights, and explore their motives and special interests. Comment on what this history reveals about American society.

2. Investigate labor unions from 1945 to the present. Explore the benefits and detriments of labor unions, the role they have played in the U.S., and their links to organized crime. Develop a thesis on the question of whether they have had a positive or negative impact on American society.

3. Investigate the underground economy of the United States since 1945. Identify the people who work "under the table" and discuss their motives. Discuss the impact of the underground economy, and why it could be both beneficial and detrimental to the economy and society's sense of law and order.

4. Research government subsidies. Report the amount of money and tax breaks that are awarded to private companies, identify the benefits of

subsidies, and explain why Congress provides these subsidies. Discuss the impact that subsidies have on small businesses and the working class. Develop a thesis on the question of whether government subsidies are good for the economy and why.

Chapter 10: Banksters and Creditmeisters

1. Investigate and develop a thesis on the claim that, "In America we have capitalism for the poor and working class, and socialism for the rich."

2. Study the Federal Reserve and discuss why its operations are often controversial. Describe its role, its accountability, its profits, and distribution of profits. Discuss the justifications of its proponents and opponents. Describe the stake the general public has in the Federal Reserve's integrity.

3. Trace the history of how corporations gained legal status as individuals since 1886 (Santa Clara County v. Southern Pacific Railroad), and discuss the implications of this status for the rich the poor, and democracy itself. Identify the key court cases, the issues at stake, and the arguments on each side of the issues. Comment on why corporate status remains controversial at present.

4. Research the history of lobbying in the U.S. and describe the events that led to its current practices and scope. Discuss the merits and detriments of lobbying, and address its impact on the distribution of wealth and democratic process. Determine whether greater regulation of lobbying is warranted.

Chapter 11: Born Again Caesar

1. Conduct a study of America's Great Awakenings. Explain why they reoccurred in history. Discuss their purpose and impact on politics and culture. Describe how the Born Again Movement of the 1970s recapitulates the Great Awakenings of the past, and identify its unique features.

2. Research the biography of either Ronald Reagan, Jimmy Carter, George H. W. Bush, Bill Clinton, or George W. Bush. Develop a thesis on whether their solicitation of conservative Christian support was sincerely motivated by love of neighbor or by exploiting the public's faith.

3. Investigate the conflict between the Arabs and Jews in the Middle East during the Cold War, and describe the American interests in the Middle East. Identify the Christian Right's agenda in the Middle East and what motivates it. Describe the extent to which oil has impacted foreign policy.

Chapter 12: A View from a Distant Shore

1. Trace the relationship of the U.S. with a Latin American country during the Cold War. Identify who initiated relations, what motivated them, and who in Latin American countries collaborated with them and why. Describe how U.S. involvement impacted indigenous people, and their progress towards democracy and economic prosperity. Develop a thesis on the question of whether the U.S. was a "good neighbor," or a predatory empire.

2. Investigate American propaganda against the Soviet Union during the Cold War as it appeared in advertising, comic books, film, and television. Describe the stereotypes of the Soviets, and determine whether the propaganda was fair and accurate. Discuss what this investigation revealed about global awareness and public opinion.

3. Research the response of the U.S. to the Hungarian uprising of 1956. Describe events that led to the uprising and what Hungarians expected from the U.S. Describe the U.S. reaction to the uprising and its consequences. Discuss what the U.S. reactions reveal about its global agenda at the time.

4. Study the role of the U.S. in Prague Spring, 1968. Describe events that led to the Czech revolt and the expectations that Czechs had regarding U.S. support. Describe the U.S. reaction to the uprising and its consequences. Discuss the U.S. response and what reveals about its global agenda at the time.

5. Compare and contrast the World War II experience of the U.S. and the Soviet Union. Consider the cost, the geo-political consequences, casualties, and the rehabilitation of society. Explain how the experiences of each nation may have shaped their perspectives of each other after the war.

6. Explore the economic relationship between the Soviet Union and the U.S. from 1945 to 1989. Identify specific business and trade agreements, and explain how these nations justified them. Discuss what these deals suggest about the ferocity of anti-Soviet propaganda and about the potential for world peace.

Chapter 13: Post-Cold War Caesar

1. Develop a thesis on the question, "Was the Cold War necessary?" Consider the source of mistrust and the ways in which the U.S. and Soviet Union collaborated on matters of trade and nuclear security. Consider the global agendas of each notion, and the opinions of statesmen on both sides who helped shape Cold War policies.

2. Develop a thesis on the question, "Did the Cold War have a positive or adverse impact on developing nations in Africa?" Consider economic, cultural, and political developments. Discuss important events and pivotal policies and their significance.

3. Describe U.S. relations with China since 1945 and identify key turning points and their significance. Discuss what shifting American policies reveal about America's anti-communism.

4. Trace the relationship of the U.S. with Saudi Arabia back to the 1930s through the present and discuss what drew the two nations together. Identify the individuals and corporations that played a role in the oil industry and how they have influenced U.S. Middle Eastern policy. Explain why some scholars are critical of U.S. Saudi relations and why others praise the relationship.

5. Study the biography of Sayyid Qutb and the roots of the Muslim Brotherhood. Describe Qutb's thesis on the West and how his ideas have fostered anti-American terrorism. Determine whether U.S. responses to Muslim complaints contributes to global tension and terrorism.

6. Investigate the Anglo-American vision for world order as was pursued by Presidents Ronald Reagan and George H. W. Bush and British Prime Minister Margaret Thatcher. Identify the key elements and objectives of their vision, and describe the values and rationality behind them. Discuss their implications for developing nations and tax payers at home.

Chapter 14: In Excelsis Deo

1. Read the report, *The Crisis of Democracy*, 1973. Identify the authors and sponsors of the report, and their agenda. Describe the thesis of the report and its implications for democracy. Address the question of whether the ideas in the report serve the general public or an unelected elite.

2. Research the role of the U.S. in the arms trade. Address the motives of corporations and the U.S. government to sell weapons internationally, and identify the benefactors of sales. Develop a thesis in response to the question: "Has the U.S. arms sales across the globe made the world a safer place?"

3. Investigate the writings of Gore Vidal and Noam Chomsky on the subject of the American empire. Explore the political ideas and social critiques they offered baby boomers, and develop a thesis in which you support or contest their assertions on the American agenda or the American character.

4. Read Don Miguel Ruiz's *The Four Agreements* and write an essay that explores whether his teachings are relevant to policy-making at home and abroad.

Chapter 4

For the Theologian/Philosopher

Caesar Ate My Jesus is meant to prompt personal reflections on one's beliefs, attitudes, values and behavior. The text challenges readers to acknowledge the human hand in the formation of scripture and doctrine, and to consider the mysticism and metaphors embedded in the Gospels. Some readers may find it difficult to imagine that the Scriptures have meaning that transcends a literal interpretation. Instructors may therefore want to prepare lessons that help students understand and appreciate various schools of exegesis, and then explain why it is fitting to consider diverse perspectives.

It is essential for instructors to create abundant time for reflections and discussions, and to ensure that reflections and discussion go beyond superficial considerations. Prompting students to think deeply means asking them to explore their feelings, hopes, fears, anxieties, ideals, cynicism, and biases. The following questions may be incorporated in to classes as individual assignments or group projects. Like the material for the historian, this material is organized by chapter, and designed to augment what has already appeared in the text.

Chapter 1: The Boom and Bust of Spirit

1. Describe the ways faith and spirituality aim to foster and nurture hope, and what happens psychologically, socially, and spiritually when people lose faith and hope.

2. Develop a thesis on the question of whether secular leaders are obligated to cultivate hope.

3. Develop a thesis regarding whether faith in God entitles the faithful to a particular standard of living and an obligation to see that other achieve it.

4. Explore the conditions you have imposed on your own love, comment on why, and on how that has impacted others' sense of dignity and hope.

Chapter 2: The Kingdom of Controversy

1. What is your own personal understanding of the Kingdom of God? How has that impacted the way you live? In what ways could you become a better "ambassador" of the Kingdom of God?

2. Describe an experience you had in which you disagreed with another person's idea of God. Take inventory of how open-minded you were and why. What does the experience teach you about your willingness to let God work in people who are different from you?

3. Read the Gnostic Gospels and comment on what they teach you about your own spirituality.

4. Compose an essay that addresses the extent to which you embrace Peter's paradigm and why.

Chapter 3: The Military Industrial Crucifix

1. Research the teachings and principles of the Just War Theory, then write an essay about where you stand on the theory and why.

2. Research the Rockefeller family's support for religious missions in Latin America, and determine whether they leavened the Kingdom of God in Latin America or did the work of Caesar.

3. Investigate the role of the Catholic Church a developing nation during the Cold War. Describe its agenda, its theological teachings, and who benefitted from their work. Determine the extent to which the Church leavened the Kingdom of God in that community.

Chapter 4: Pope John Kennedy

1. Examine *Pacem in Terris*, 1963, (Pope John XXIII) and describe the Catholic Church's position on peace, prosperity, and nuclear weapons. Discuss whether you agree with Pope John XXIII and why.

2. Discuss a time when you dissented from an authority's position on an issue. Describe the interests at stake and how you articulated your dissent. Discuss your risks, how others respond to you, the role of your faith or spirituality in the event, and what you learned about dissent from the experience.

3. Read John F. Kennedy's American University Commencement Speech (June, 1963), and comment on whether the rhetoric resembles an appeal to a tribal god, or is something more prophetic.

Chapter 5: The Quicksand of Vietnam

1. Interview a veteran of war and write about how the war experience impacted the veteran's sense of human dignity, empathy for others, and belief in God. Discuss your reaction to the interview.

2. View the National Geographic film, "Vietnam: Unseen War" which looks at how photographers and the Vietnamese saw the war. Develop a thesis in response to the following statement: "It is the moral obligation of journalists to reveal the truth about war as it is being waged."

3. Meditate on those Americans have labeled "our enemies," and the way they are depicted in the media. Study the "enemy's" discontent and criticism of the U.S. and explore to extent to which you are able empathize with the "enemy." Discuss your journey towards empathy for your adversaries.

Chapter 6: Dissent

1. Read the essays of Thomas Merton against the war in Vietnam and discuss whether his arguments apply to the "War against Terrorism" and why.

2. Read Thich Nhat Hanh's *Vietnam: Lotus in a Sea of Fire* (1967). Discuss the author's Buddhist proposal for peace and what it reveals about man's

struggle with ego, power, and vanity. Comment on whether Thich Nhat Hanh's approach to peace is an articulation of the Kingdom of God and why.

3. Read the speeches and essays of elected officials who opposed the war (such as Ron Dellums, J. William Fulbright, Eugene McCarthy, Bella Abzug, Albert Gore, Sr., George McGovern, and Wayne Morse), and describe how they leavened the Kingdom of God into their work.

4. Read the essays and speeches of of those who supported the war (such as Midge Decter, Senator Everet Dirksen, Henry Kissinger, and Barry Goldwater) and describe what they believed was a moral obligation to fight.

5. Read the essays and speeches of those who initially supported the war in Vietnam, (such as Clark Clifford, Robert McNamara, Daniel Ellsberg, and Senator J. William Fulbright) then changed their minds as the war escalated. Explore what caused these individuals to change their minds, and what lessons can be learned from their experiences about steering the course of one's own conscience.

Chapter 7: Civil Rights

1. Meditate on your thoughts, feelings, and attitudes regarding race and racism. Compose an essay that addresses your own journey with racism, and describe how the journey speaks to your spirituality.

2. Meditate on who or which groups have been the "Isaacs" in your own life, and describe how you justified the sacrifice of their needs, well-being, and dignity. Explore your journey to love the "least" of your brothers and sisters and comment on your progress.

Chapter 8: Sex and the Kingdom

1. Discuss what sexual dignity means, and describe how you developed this concept. Explore how social norms and spirituality impact your respect for the opposite sex and people with sexual orientations different from your own.

2. Respond to the statement: "This a man's world and our spirituality potential is limited because men believe that love and empathy are signs of weakness."

3. Determine whether the consumption of pornography is injurious to one's spirituality.

4. Identify the characteristics of the ideal family and why those characteristics are important to you.

Chapter 9: The Dignity of Labor

1. Interview someone who has been homeless and compose an essay that describes the circumstances that led to the homelessness and the impact of homelessness on the individual's sense of dignity and hope. Explore whether you harbor judgment and bigotry against the homeless and why.

2. The author asserts that it is a sin to make people feel worthless and to treat people like objects in the workplace. Discuss your thoughts about this and whether society has a moral obligation to sustain full employment and why.

3. Meditate on the question of the extent to which you rely on what you do for a living to represent your character and value to the world. Determine whether this brings you closer to the Kingdom of God or to your own ego and why.

Chapter 10: Banksters and Creditmeisters

1. Develop a thesis in response to the following statement: "The economy is an amoral entity that is driven by supply and demand, and society has no moral obligation to interfere with that process."

2. Inventory your standard of living and take account of the possessions and services you take for granted. Develop a plan whereby you reduce your cost of living. Then, discuss what changes you may have to make in your values to do so, and address the spiritual benefits of doing so.

3. Read *Economic Justice for All* (Conference of Catholic Bishops in the United States, 1986) and identify the ways in which this document challenges Prosperity Theology, as articulated by Joel Osteen, Creflo Dollar, and Kenneth Copeland. Discuss your beliefs about whether gaining and using wealth have sacred properties.

Chapter 11: Born-Again Caesar

1. Read *How Would Jesus Vote?* (James Kennedy and Jerry Newcombe, 2008) and compose and essay that develops your reaction to its thesis. Determine whether Kennedy and Newcombe's perception of Jesus is prophetic or priestly in nature, and whether their directives enhance society's spirituality.

2. Read Pat Robertson's *The New World Order* (1991). Discuss whether you agree with his view of the world, and comment on whether his thesis represents the Kingdom of God and why.

3. Compose an essay based on the following question: "Would you describe your theological outlook as prophetic or priestly, and what evidence would you offer to support the claim?"

Chapter 12: A View from a Distant Shore

1. Meditate on an experience in which you were humbled by an embarrassing thing you said or did. Describe what happened and what the experience taught you about your ego and empathy.

2. Describe conversation you had with a person from another country in which they criticized the U.S. Comment on your reaction and what it reveals about your love of neighbor.

Chapter 13: Post-Cold War Caesar

1. Develop a thesis based on the statement: "The U.S. has a moral obligation to make the world in its own image because the U.S. best understands how to use wealth and power for good."

2. Describe the criteria you use to vote for candidates for public office and whether the candidate's faith and moral character impact your judgement and why.

Chapter 14: In Excelsis Deo

1. Compose an essay based on the following question: "Would you describe yourself as a more hopeful, or a more cynical on the matter of confidence in humanity's capacity to bring the Kingdom of God to bear on earth, and why?"

2. Describe your experience with "messianic fatigue." Explore the role of your ego and expectations. Discuss how it is possible to set boundaries while serving those in need.

3. Think of someone in your life who supported you at a critical time in your life when you were ready to throw your spirituality away. Describe the experience and what you learned from it.

4. Read Don Miguel Ruiz's *The Four Agreements* and discuss how you might apply the lessons in your own personal life.

5. Take inventory of how you spend time in an average week, and identify which hours are largely spent on Caesar's treadmill. Be honest about the time you spend consuming media and what kinds of media you consume; be honest about the time and money you spend on vanity items and unessential possessions. Discuss whether your life would be improved by spending more time in meditation, prayer, learning, or nurturing relationships.

Chapter 5

The Prepared Instructor

Purpose and Rationale

As *Caesar Ate My Jesus* references information from multiple disciplines, instructors may want to read the book a couple of times through and identify lacunae in their own knowledge about history, the Catholic Church and its documents, economics, American culture, or foreign affairs. Anticipating and being ready to respond to students' gaps in these areas is important. The instructor may also decide that the best way to ensure student comprehension is to have a pre-requisite for the course. Pre-requisites might include courses in American and Church history.

The prepared instructor has identified the learning outcomes or the point of undertaking exercises and conversations. The well-prepared instructor distinguishes outcomes that are academic, cognitive, affective, and formative. Effective instructors understand that assessing students' work is sometimes a matter of refining the quality of students' thoughtfulness, and not a matter of recalling facts or parroting the instructor's perspectives. They communicate the purpose of each session, use transparent and appropriate criteria for student evaluations, and are able to anticipate the challenges students might face as they grapple with new materials and perspectives.

The prepared instructor determines well ahead of the first day of class which ancillary materials are appropriate for instruction. This might include films and a reading list based on key publications (see Appendix B). Further, the prepared instructor has considered the extent to which instruction will engage students in the community, and has made contact with off-campus agencies and organizations to secure permission for students to contact their representative for interviews, or for completing service-learning requirements.

The issues, events, and ideas presented in *Caesar Ate My Jesus* may trigger very emotional responses from students. It may be helpful to establish some "rules of engagement" at the beginning of the course. These might include guidelines about respectful language, boundaries about self-disclosure, confidentiality regarding things said in class, respect for the reputation of others, and paying attention while others are speaking, rather than being distracted with electronic devices or other work.

Coping with Controversy

A well-prepared instructor is also aware of his or her biases about the issues, events, and ideas found in the sources used for instruction. Depending on how it is handled, the instructor's bias can be a "teachable moment," and these must be approached with discretion. Consider the following statements made by three different instructors who each found themselves in the middle of a class discussion about a belief that students held strongly, but one that the instructor had always opposed with a passion.

> **Professor Maples:** "I think we need to call a time out on this discussion, and spend some more time looking at the facts."

> **Professor Elms:** "This is very typical of your generation, you guys have to remember that passion doesn't make you right. You need to move towards a more matured view of the world."

> **Professor Spruce:** "I am glad that many of you have shared your thoughts on this. I admit that this issue is difficult for me and I struggle with your consensus because I am not sure whether certain assumptions are true for me. I need to think more about this before I respond."

Note that the instructors do not reveal their positions on the matter, yet each has communicated something very important to the students. Professor Maples' statement implied that students did not have enough information to proceed in a reasonable way. This may or may not have been honest, but it did shift the conversation away from a difficult matter. Maples is risking that students will think that he or she believes that they have not done their homework or are too ignorant for dialogue.

Professor Elms may have had a very authentic reaction to the debate, but its pedagogical value is compromised by the potential ha he or she may have violated students' trust by openly insulting them. The fact that Elms has power over the students' grades may intimidate students who will no longer risk sharing their ideas and experiences because they assume they will be personally judged for them.

Professor Spruce began with a statement of gratitude and acknowledged that the issue was a tough one. Spruce's comments confirm the reality that sometimes truth and rightness are ambiguous. Spruce left open the possibility that the class could further explore the issues later, and confirmed the reality that the issues were serious enough to warrant further consideration.

It is vital to leave students an honorable way out of conflict. In class discussions this might be accomplished by raising a question that would illuminate alternative perspectives or pathways to consensus. It may be accomplished by addressing what it means to honorably and respectfully agree to disagree. The key to having students learn from conflict is to avoid sliding over it or ignoring it, and to resist the temptation to make it a personal issue. Teaching others how to face conflict, volatility, and ultimatums is another way of preparing students for their interactions in the real world. These lessons may even be linked to conversations about humility and he ego, which are both explicitly addressed in *Caesar Ate My Jesus*.

Chapter 6

For the Retreat Facilitator

Spiritual retreats often blend learning with rituals, reflection, and social interaction. Effective facilitation of these events ensures that the activities are purposeful and bound together by a clear and relevant theme. Effective facilitators help participants stay focused on activities and remain fair in their use of time, as to allow everyone sufficient time to express themselves and make needed inquiries. They create environments in which people feel safe to share their thoughts and feelings. This is sometimes accomplished by the use of icebreakers, such as the one described earlier in *Chapter 1* of this guide.

Themes

Caesar Ate My Jesus explores many themes that are germane to the human experience with faith and spirituality. All themes readily lend themselves to the inclusion of reconciliation ceremonies, communal prayer, and thanksgiving. It is very helpful to have retreat participants read the book or key sections of it prior to the retreat. Facilitators should be well-acquainted with the book so that questions about its assertions can be addressed accurately and fairly.

The following sample sessions follow some of the same pedagogical rules as classroom instruction, which is to say the facilitator will present the objectives for the retreat and invite participants to explore some ground rules that will help everyone stay focused and respectful. It is also helpful for facilitators to alert participants to the schedule, and to signal participants when time matters. This might consist of telling people that in the group discussion or a pair-share following reflection, each person has about two minutes to state their thoughts. It might be that facilitators will ring a bell that indicates that folks have about five minutes to wrap up their reflections or group work. The following are samples of retreats based on themes that integrate material and ideas from *Caesar Ate My Jesus.*

Sample I: Welcoming Spiritual Renewal

The purpose of this session is to share experiences of doubt and spiritual frustration and explore the reasons why it is not, as the author says, time to "throw the spiritual baby out" (p. 11). This retreat also aims to raise participants' awareness of strategies they can use on a daily basis to cope with uncertainty and cynicism. In this retreat, participants will:

1. Share experiences with doubt and spiritual frustration

2. Explore sacred teachings concerning the conflict between spiritual ideals and earthly life

3. Reflect on personal expectations related to spirituality and life and whether they are reasonable

4. Discuss various perspectives on appropriate expectations for spirituality

5. Explore the role ego plays in personal expectations relative to spirituality

6. Explore the dangers of assimilating the expectations of others that do not resonate with one's sense of love and respectful connection to others

7. Identify meaningful and tenable goals for renewing one's spirituality

8. Reflect on the differences between sentimentality and spirituality (*Caesar,* pp. 248–249) and consider the possibility that ego makes spirituality harder than what it has to be

9. Watch the film "*Is a Wonderful Life,*" and participate in group discussion, wherein individuals share their thoughts on which characters remind them of themselves, and why, and to address the reality in their own lives that one never knows what difference one might make

10. Participate in a prayer circle in which individuals meditate on and express gratitude for the spiritual resources that are immediately accessible in their lives

Sample II: Facing Caesar

The purpose of this session is to take a personal inventory of the ways in which we have assimilated Caesar and to consider the impact that this had had on others and our own lives. It is an opportunity to scrutinize our values, wants, and assumptions about what is good for us. It is also to engage in reconciliation with others and address the way individuals can keep Caesar at a distance. Participants in this study will:

1. Identify "Caesar's" agenda, values, and characteristics, and how they differ from the Kingdom of God and the teachings of Jesus (*Caesar*, p. 7–8).

2. Take a personal inventory to clarify personal attitudes and beliefs (Appendix C).

3. Share the results of the inventory with another person in a pair-share and be prepared to share the results and thoughts on them in a group discussion (see follow-up questions in Appendix B).

4. Meditate on the role of fear, ignorance, and ego might be playing in your spiritual life and how these things impact your journey towards the Kingdom of God and keep you close to Caesar.

5. Create a plan to get off of Caesar's treadmill, which might address the way you spend money and time, the way you worry about status and looks, or the way you relate to others at work and at home.

6. Share ideas about getting off Caesar's treadmill with others and discuss what will aid your success.

7. Participate in a prayer service devoted to renewing one's commitment to the Kingdom of God.

Sample III: Healing Isaac

The purpose of this session is to explore the ways we have made Isaacs of others and the ways in which others have made Isaacs of us (in the way Isaac is understood in *Caesar*, p. 34–35), and to explore the things that keep us committed to the idea some people by nature are the "least of our brothers." This session also aims to explore the value of self-esteem in spirituality.

1. Identify the people in your life who cause you to feel disgust or who arouse severe judgment.

2. Explore the reasons why certain individuals arouse anger and severe judgment and determine the extent to which your ego is invested in the anger or judgement, or why you feel threatened.

3. In pair-share, talk about a time when you sacrificed someone's reputation, privacy, well-being, advancement, opportunity, health, or dignity, what motivated you, what became of the experience, and what it taught you about yourself.

4. In pair-share, talk about a time in which somebody made you an Isaac by sacrificing your reputation, privacy, advancement, well-being, opportunity, health, or dignity. Address how you felt about yourself and the other person. Explore the spiritual lessons offered by the experience.

5. Explore what Jesus and other spiritual teachers, such as Martin Luther King Jr., Mohandas K. Gandhi, or Sr. Helen Prejean teach us about the persecution of the least of our brothers and sisters.

6. Participate in a group discussion about strategies to make amends with the Isaacs in our lives.

7. Participate in group discussion about strategies to make amends with those who have made Isaacs of us, and to honor our own dignity.

8. Participate in a reconciliation ceremony that is aimed at renewing one's commitment to love the least of our brothers and sisters.

Sample IV: How Big is My God Box?

The objective of this session is to explore our personal beliefs about God, who has access to God, how we define legitimate approaches to God and spiritual living, and what consequences our beliefs might have for our life and relationships with others. The activities aim to help individuals clarify the paradigms by which they live and why. Participants should be familiar with the material in Chapter 2: The Kingdom of Controversy (*Caesar*, pp. 15–31). Participants will:

1. Explore the difference between Peter's paradigm and alternative approaches to the identity of Jesus, such as the Gnostic approach to the identity of Jesus, and explore how such approaches color the interpretation of Jesus' teaching, crucifixion, and resurrection.

2. Explore the function of Peter's paradigm in orthodox Christianity and its benefits and detriments.

3. Reflect on a time when you judged or openly criticized a person's beliefs about God or Jesus, what motivated your response, and consider whether the experience brought either person closer to the Kingdom of God and why. Consider the author's personal experience in *Caesar* (p. 209).

4. In pair-share, talk about an experience in which someone criticized your spirituality and explore its impact on your willingness to trust and love others.

5. Participate in group discussion in which everyone explores their motivations for judging other's approach to God, examines the anxiety we may have about how others think about God.

6. Participate in meditation and group discussion that explores the ways to overcome judgment and anxiety about what others think.

7. Reflect on the statement, "To sustain my credentials as a 'born-again' Christian, I had to narrow God's access to me. It was not acceptable to welcome the spiritual wisdom of Native Americans, Jews, Buddhists, or atheists. God was treated like the exclusive property of Christian evangelicals, and that in itself makes God an idol, not God." (*Caesar*, p. 249) The author suggests that orthodoxy tends to confine God to the role a supernatural tribal chieftain, and that this makes an idol of God. Discuss whether Americans have rightly or wrongly claimed that God favors America above all.

8. Meditate on the quotation, "Like all man-made religious institutions, the church stands for something that transcends its own doctrines" (p. 14), and discuss what this might mean to your own spirituality.

9. Participate in a prayer ceremony in which we commit ourselves to being open to the ways in which God works in unexpected ways through people we might not like very much.

Appendix A

Sample Pre-Test for a Course
Using *Caesar Ate My Jesus*

Directions: Select the response that best answers the question. Be prepared to explore the correct answers in class and to take notes on the material.

1. What was the Cold War?

    a. An era in history defined by conflict between the U.S. and Soviet Union

    b. A race to see whether the U.S. or Nazi Germany would get atomic weapons first

    c. The period of time in which the U.S. occupied Japan after World War II

    d. A period defined by America's struggle to overcome its racism and discrimination

2. What is the difference between communism and capitalism?

    a. Communism supports public investment in private businesses, capitalism does not

    b. Communism does not hold elections for public office, capitalism does

    c. Communism supports a state-run, centralized economy, capitalism does not

    d. Communism exploits the working class, capitalism does not

3. How did the Cold War impact developing nations in Africa and Latin America?

    a. It intensified wars of independence as the US and Soviet Union competed for influence

    b. It led to the mass industrialization and modernization of those regions

    c. It resulted in large numbers of atomic weapons installation in those regions

    d. It had little to no impact because they were poor nations

4. How did the Cold War impact Americans at home?

    a. The government investigated Hollywood writers' and actors' political views

    b. The government passed laws that called for the incarceration of communists

    c. Teachers and public servants were forced to take a loyalty oath to keep their jobs

    d. All of the above

5. What was America's economy like after World War II and why?

    a. It was robust as U.S. industries were not destroyed in war and Allies owed it money

    b. It was stable but profoundly weakened by the cost of fighting in the war

    c. It was in a state of Great Depression in which many were out of work

    d. It was growing rapidly and the U.S reached nearly zero percent poverty and unemployment

6. Bonds, mutual funds and credit default swaps are collectively known as:

    a. Stocks

    b. Financial Products

    c. Certificates of Deposit

    d. Marginal Growth Receipts

7. What does it mean to "monetize" debt?

    a. It means treating money owed to a bank like real cash in hand that can be invested

    b. It means to impose very heavy taxes on checking accounts and credit cards

    c. It means using the money nations owe other nations to calculate their risk for loans

    d. It means excusing corporations with government contracts from paying taxes

8. In 1950, the percent of non-whites in the U.S. was _____ and by 2010 it was _____:

    a. About 12% . . . nearly 30%

    b. About 8% . . . nearly 35%

    c. About 5% . . . nearly 20%

    d. About 3% . . . nearly 25%

9. Which statement is false regarding CIA activity during the Cold War?

    a. It investigated the private lives of civil rights workers and ant-war demonstrators

    b. It orchestrated the overthrow of legally elected officials in foreign countries

    c. It destroyed almost all drug trafficking and production in Asia and Latin America

    d. It used religious ministers as spies and agents

10. In 1962, _____ percent of Americans were Christian, and by 2012, _____ were Christian.

    a. 98% and 74%

    b. 93% and 77%

    c. 89% and 65%

    d. 83% and 59%

11. What does it mean to interpret sacred scriptures, like the Gospels, in a metaphoric way?

   a. It means taking each word as the exact word God as God revealed it

   b. It is a way of understanding language that illuminates something transcendent

   c. It is a process of cross-referencing passages to determine the accuracy of text

   d. It is a form of reading that focuses on the context in which something was written

12. America has experienced many "Great Awakenings;" what are they?

   a. They are social reform movements that appeal to reason in order to serve justice

   b. They are periods during which technological innovation leaps forward quickly

   c. They are events in which ground-breaking legislation and court decisions are made

   d. They are Christian fundamentalist revivals calling for people to be born again

Answers with Notes

1. (A) The Cold War lasted from 1945 to 1991. Despite the fact that the U.S. and Soviet Union were allies in World War II, the U.S. renewed its animosity towards communism after the Soviet Union "appropriated" the Eastern Blok nations, and the Soviet Union renewed its dislike for the U.S. as the U.S. had a monopoly on atomic weapons and supported imperialism around the globe.

2. (C) The U.S. government has given public money to private corporations by way of tax breaks and subsidies to pay for marketing and development.

3. (A) The Cold War saw the U.S. and Soviet Union compete for influence in nations emerging from colonialism after World War II. They both sold weapons to indigenous populations and supported a dictators who gave them with access to natural resources and strategic locations for military bases. Efforts industrialize developing nations did not result in full equality with industrial nations.

4. (D) Between 1938 and 1975, The House Committee on Un-American Activities (HUAC) investigated communism in American. The Senate Internal Security Committee also investigated communist threats to the U.S. Its famous chairman, Senator Joseph McCarthy (R-WI), was ultimately disgraced for his zealotry. HUAC targeted Hollywood as it feared that films might contain communist propaganda. Labors unions, liberal associations, and members of the government and military fell under scrutiny. The Internal Security Act of 1950 required communist organizations to register with the Attorney General's office, and called for the detention of those suspected of espionage or sabotage. Many protested as they felt investigations violated the right to free speech.

5. (A) The U.S. economy after World War II was strong, as the U.S. mainland and its industries were not destroyed during the war. The U.S. made money selling supplies to its allies. The economies of Britain, Germany, and Japan were in ruins as their industries and cities were bombed. The U.S. economy slipped into a series of recessions and inflation in the late 1960s and 1970s. Despite the strength of the U.S. economy, the unemployment rate between 1946 and 1960 averaged about 5%; and, while the poverty rate dramatically decreased during that time, it remained above 20% throughout the 1950s.

6. (B) Financial products are all investment opportunities that bear various degrees of risk. Some may be insured, and investors are thus compensated even when investments fail.

7. (A) Monetizing debt is very risky investment practice, because when debts are not repaid, the original lender *and* the person who used the debt as money to invest both lose their capital.

8. (A) The U.S. has become more diverse since 1945. This is challenging as people struggle to create a consensus on what it means to be a good citizen and yet avoid being disrespectful to diverse cultures.

9. (C) The CIA was formed in 1947 and has served the national security and the private sector's interests in the expansion of business. To fund its covert activities, the CIA has engaged in drug and arms trafficking. This enables it to operate without accountability to Congress. See: *Crossing the Rubicon* (Michale Ruppert, 2004) and *Cocaine Politics* (Peter S. Dale, 1998).

10. (B) Shifts in religious affiliations since 1945 have aroused concerns for the well-being of America, especially since the 9/11 attacks in the U.S. and subsequent acts of terrorism around the world.

11. (B) The literal interpretation of the Bible regards each word as that spoken or revealed by God. A contextual reading of scriptures takes into account the time, place, the author's purpose, and the cultural milieu in which the scriptures were received. Metaphors are often used to convey the transcendent or mystical properties of something. To say for example, that somebody *is* a cheetah means something different from saying that somebody runs *like* a cheetah. The simile is captured in the use of the word "like," but to say that one *is* a cheetah is to suggest that the person is—though not in form—in essence, in keenness of his senses, body control, and way of being in the world, a cheetah. To read scripture metaphorically opens the possibility that the truth may lie beyond the literal word. This is especially important when applied to the identity of Jesus. Was Jesus literally God, or was the title a metaphor?

12. (D) Great Awakenings have reoccurred in U.S. history, and are usually preceded by a period of social upheaval. They are characterized by preaching about morality, a literal reading of scripture, eschatological declarations, and a call to accept Jesus as one's personal savior. The Born-Again movement of the 1960s and 1970s occurred in the wake of mass protests and cultural upheaval.

Appendix B

Scholarly Journals

America [Catholic. Established by Jesuits in 1909, the magazine reports Catholic news and provides essays and opinions about world events with Catholic commentary.]

American Communist History [Since 2002, the Historians of American Communism have offered this journal, which examines American communism and America's response to socialism and the American Left.]

American Jewish History [Founded in 1892 by the American Jewish Historical Society, this journal explores the Jewish culture, the Jewish experience in America, and he Jewish perspective on issues and events.]

American Quarterly [Since 1949, the American Studies Association has published his peer-reviewed journal that examines history, politics, ethics, and culture.]

Christianity in Crisis [Established in 1941 by Reinhold Niebuhr, folded in 1993. The journal represented Christian liberal thinking and explored matters of politics and social justice.]

Christianity Today [Protestant. Established in 1956 with direction from Reverend Billy Graham, to provide balanced reporting on world events with biblical commentary, and to evangelize.]

Cold War History [Established in 2000 in London, this is a peer-reviewed journal that examines the events of and personalities involved in the Cold War.]

Diplomatic History [Established in 1977 by the Historians of American Foreign Relations, explores international relations.]

Economic History Review [Established in 1927, this journal examines world history with an eye to the production, distribution, and impact of material goods on society.]

Ethics [Founded in 1890, this journal explores political, economic, and philosophical issues from diverse perspectives.]

Ethics and International Affairs [Begun in 1989 and published by the Carnegie Council on Ethics and International Affairs, his journal offers commentary on the moral aspects of international conflicts, propaganda, and human rights.]

Foreign Affairs [Founded in 1922, this magazine explores diplomacy and international relations through the lens of the Foreign Affairs Council, a nonpartisan think tank founded by bankers, international investors, journalists, and statesmen.]

Journal of American History [Founded in 1907 by the Mississippi Valley Historical Association, this peer-reviewed journal investigates history, biography, and historiography in order to advance the teaching of American history]

Journal of American Studies [Since 1967, the British Association of American Studies has examined the concept of "America" through critical studies of its culture, governance, and literature, and politics.]

Journal of Cold War Studies [Founded in 1999 by MIT, this journal contains peer-reviewed articles on the former Communist world and examines history and diplomacy in light of de-classified archives.]

Journal of Conflict Resolution [First published in 1957, this journal examines the practical, theoretical and ethical dimension of conflict-resolution in society and international relations.]

Journal of Economic History [Published by Cambridge University Press since 1941, his journal examines social history through the lens of economic policies and experiences.]

Journal of Ethics [This international review was established in the Netherlands in 1997, and explores morality and ethics as they concern politics, culture, and society.]

Journal of Genocide Research [Established in 1999 by the International Network of Genocide scholars, his journal publishes essays exploring he Holocaust, other genocides, and the way history treats them.]

Journal of Global Ethics [Examines globalism and global issues with emphasis on ethics in practice.]

Journal of Military History [Since 1937, the Society for Military History has refereed this publication which offered essays about national defense, war-making, and the experience of war.]

Journal of Peace Research [Published bi-annually since 1964 by the Peace Research Institute in Oslo, Norway, this journal examines imperialism, war, diplomacy, violence, peace, and public perceptions.]

Journal of Poverty and Social Justice [Published by the University of Leeds, UK since 1992, this journal examines the causes of poverty, legislation and policies concerning he poor, poverty's impact on minorities and women, and the welfare state, and is international in scope.]

Journal of Religious History [This Australian publication began in 1960, and addresses the way religion has interacted with society, politics, and economics over many centuries world-wide.]

Journal of Social History [George Mason University began publishing his journal in 1967, and explores society with interest in demographic and consumer trends, social values and attitudes, and popular culture. It is international in scope and examines many centuries.]

Journal of Women's History [This quarterly has been published since 1989 by Johns Hopkins University, and examines women's experience across the globe and centuries. Many perspectives of feminism are represented.]

Labor History [Since 1953, this peer-reviewed quarterly has offered studies of international events and conditions and their impact on economic systems, labor, and the poor and working class.]

National Catholic Reporter [Catholic. Established in 1964 to increase coverage of Catholic issues and perspectives.]

Past and Present [Founded by an association of Marxists and non-Marxists in 1952. This British journal examines history from international liberal perspectives.]

Radical History Review [Established in 1975 to explore culture, politics, and economics from the perspective of the working class and marginalized populations.]

Ramparts Magazine [New Left. Established by liberal Catholic, Edward Keating in 1962, the magazine folded in 1975. It published literary works and essays by noted theologians and activists.]

Social Justice [Established in 1974 to inform theory and practice on matters related to crime, equality, and justice.]

The American Historical Review [Established in 1895, the quarterly prints scholarly essays about history.]

The Catholic Historical Review [Since 1915, the Catholic Historical Association has published this journal, which offers studies of the Catholic Church since its formation, is international in scope, and which undertakes social, political, and economic issues.]

Vital Speeches [Founded in 1934 for the purpose of preserving and disseminating speeches made by leaders, scientists, humanitarians, and scholars.]

Appendix C

Assimilation of Caesar Inventory

The Inventory

The purpose of this inventory is to prompt self-awareness and generate conversation about why we believe what we believe, and to consider the impact of our beliefs on our spiritual development and relationships with others. There are no right or wrong responses to these statements.

Use this Likert scale to represent your responses to each statement: 1=Strongly Disagree 2=Mildly Disagree 3=Equally Disagree and Agree 4=Mildly Agree 5=Strongly Agree

1. People should obey government officials because God placed them in office   1 2 3 4 5

2. Owning businesses and property enhances one's sense of social responsibility   1 2 3 4 5

3. Having empathy for our enemies arouses unrealistic expectations for good will   1 2 3 4 5

4. One's prosperity is solely the result of the individual's effort and discipline   1 2 3 4 5

5. Christians should tolerate injustice because they will be rewarded in Heaven   1 2 3 4 5

6. Complete transparency of economic practice threatens national security   1 2 3 4 5

7. Perfect equality before he law is a nice idea, but in reality it is dangerous   1 2 3 4 5

8. Without strict adherence to religious rules, people ultimately become immoral

1 2 3 4 5

9. It is better to respect popular consensus than to dissent for the sake of spiritual ideals

1 2 3 4 5

10. In order to save the world, Christians must do whatever they need to do to survive

1 2 3 4 5

Add the scores and divide the total by ten to render an average score. Differences between your average and individual item scores and those of others may help you understand the dynamics that affect one's relationships. Averages between 5 and 4.5 suggest a strong alignment with "Caesar" and averages between 1 and 1.5 suggest a strong rejection of "Caesar." In this inventory, Caesar's world view is characterized by a strong preference for individualism, political realism, materialism, a mistrust of personal conscience, and confidence in the wisdom of an elite. Religion in "Caesar's" world tends to represents a means of maintaining order and the status quo, and is typically more priestly than prophetic in is approach to faith and morality.

Follow-up

These questions might be discussed in pairs with the intention of facilitating personal reflection, or they can be discussed in large groups for the purpose of learning more about our own individual values and the extent to which we are influenced by society, and the extent to which we own our own conscience.

1. Which question was the easiest to answer and why?

2. Which question was the most difficult to answer and why?

3. Would you say that people who know you well would agree with all your responses? What does this reveal about the way others see you and the way you see yourself?

4. Would you say that your responses to these assertions reflect attitudes you acquired through prayer and meditation or through social assimilation? Why difference might that make?

www.ingramcontent.com/pod-product-compliance
Lightning Source LLC
LaVergne TN
LVHW050047090426
835511LV00033B/2797